SCIENCE ACADEMY
ELECTRIC EMERGENCY

BY KIRSTY HOLMES

CRABTREE
PUBLISHING COMPANY
WWW.CRABTREEBOOKS.COM

CRABTREE
PUBLISHING COMPANY
WWW.CRABTREEBOOKS.COM

Author:
 Kirsty Holmes
Editorial director:
 Kathy Middleton
Editors:
 Madeline Tyler, Janine Deschenes
Proofreader:
 Petrice Custance
Graphic design:
 Ian McMullen
Prepress technician:
 Katherine Berti
Print coordinator:
 Katherine Berti

All images are courtesy of Shutterstock.com, unless otherwise specified. With thanks to Getty Images, Thinkstock Photo, and iStockphoto.

Front Cover: Cookie Studio, AlexRoz, Twin Design, Devita ayu silvianingtyas, Pixfiction, Africa Studio, Alexapicso, Somchai Som, ffolas, Tapui, VectorPot

Interior: Background – TheBestGraphics. Arrows – Sasha Ka. Characters: Lewis – Cookie Studio. Dee Dee – LightField Studios. Kush: Gratsias Adhi Hermawan. Ling: GOLFX. Paige: Oleksandr Zamuruiev. Katie: LightField Studios. BudE – sdecoret. Professor Adams – HBRH. 6 – Machine: Iaremenko Sergii.12 – Macrovector. 13 – Diyana Dimitrova. WDG Photo. Gary Saxe. N.Minton. 14 – FabrikaSimf. 16 – Ice_AisberG. 17 –FabrikaSimf. Yeti studio. Jr images. 18 – Rad K. Bernd Juergens. Ms S. Ann. rbkomar. Barnaby Chambers. Rainer Fuhrmann. 19 –Snova. 20-21 – Unkas Photo. Tartila. Tomsickova Tatyana. Gwoeii. Vanessa Volk. Jane Rix. Corepics VOF. 22– Africa Studio. 23 – atiana Popova. Purple Clouds. Damir Khabirov. Krivosheev Vitaly. Sergey Peterman. mama_mia

All facts, statistics, web addresses, and URLs in this book were verified as valid and accurate at time of writing. No responsibility for any changes to external websites or references can be accepted by either the author or publisher.

Library and Archives Canada Cataloguing in Publication

Title: Electric emergency / by Kirsty Holmes.
Names: Holmes, Kirsty, author.
Description: Series statement: Science academy | Originally published: King's Lynn: BookLife, 2020. | Includes index.
Identifiers: Canadiana (print) 2020035776X | Canadiana (ebook) 20200357778 | ISBN 9781427130549 (hardcover) | ISBN 9781427130587 (softcover) | ISBN 9781427130624 (HTML)
Subjects: LCSH: Electricity—Juvenile literature. | LCSH: Power (Mechanics)—Juvenile literature.
Classification: LCC QC527.2 .H65 2021 | DDC j537—dc23

Library of Congress Cataloging-in-Publication Data

Names: Holmes, Kirsty, author.
Title: Electric emergency / by Kirsty Holmes.
Description: New York : Crabtree Publishing Company, 2021. | Series: Science academy | Includes index. | Audience: Ages 6-9 | Audience: Grades 2-3 | Summary: "Help! The 3-D pizza printer is not working. Join the students at Science Academy as they solve their lunchtime problem while Professor Adams explains how electricity works and where it comes from. Simple sentences and easy-to-understand examples make learning about electricity understandable and fun"-- Provided by publisher.
Identifiers: LCCN 2020045832 (print) | LCCN 2020045833 (ebook) | ISBN 9781427130549 (hardcover) | ISBN 9781427130587 (paperback) | ISBN 9781427130624 (ebook)
Subjects: LCSH: Electricity--Juvenile literature.
Classification: LCC QC527.2 .H654 2021 (print) | LCC QC527.2 (ebook) | DDC 537--dc23
LC record available at https://lccn.loc.gov/2020045832
LC ebook record available at https://lccn.loc.gov/2020045833

Crabtree Publishing Company

www.crabtreebooks.com   1–800–387–7650
Published by Crabtree Publishing Company in 2021
© 2020 BookLife Publishing Ltd.

Published in Canada
Crabtree Publishing
616 Welland Ave.
St. Catharines, Ontario
L2M 5V6

Published in the United States
Crabtree Publishing
347 Fifth Ave
Suite 1402-145
New York, NY 10016

Printed in the U.S.A./122020/CG20201014

CONTENTS

Words that are bold, like **this**, can be found in the glossary on page 24.

Another day at Science Academy has begun. Time to take attendance! Meet class 201.

Lewis
Favorite subject:
Electricity

Dee Dee
Favorite subject:
Movement

Katie
Favorite subject:
Pulling forces

Ling
Favorite subject:
Pushing forces

Paige
Favorite subject:
Magnets

Ravi
Favorite subject:
Energy

Today's lesson is all about a type of energy called electricity. The students will learn answers to these questions:

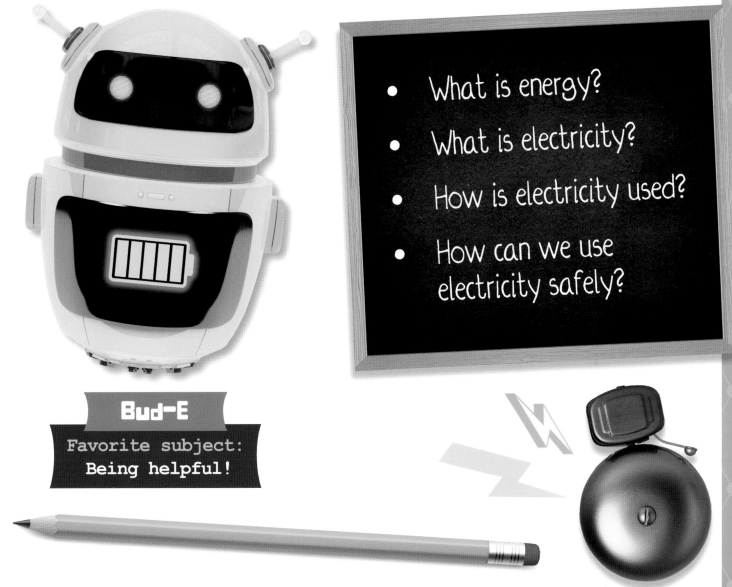

- What is energy?
- What is electricity?
- How is electricity used?
- How can we use electricity safely?

Bud-E

Favorite subject:
Being helpful!

Science Academy is a school especially for kids who love science and solving problems! Do I hear the bell?

It has been a busy morning. The class has been making a very special machine: a **3-D printer** that makes pizza! It's time to test the machine to see if it works as it should. All they have to do is turn it on.

3-D printer

When the classmates try to turn on the 3-D printer, there is a pop and a bang! Instead of printing a pizza, the pizza printer stays still. It does not work at all. Professor Adams looks confused.

What happened to the printer? Something must have gone wrong.

LUNCHTIME

The classmates look around. Many other classroom objects are also not working! The lights have shut off. The computers will not turn on. It is lunchtime, but the bell did not ring. Professor Adams says it must be a power outage.

What's a power outage?

It means that there is no electricity coming into the school at all!

Electricity is a type of energy. Energy is the power to do work. Many machines need electricity to work. Lights, computers, microwaves, and ovens all need electricity. Wait...if microwaves and ovens do not work, how will the cafeteria serve lunch?

What? No pizza and now no lunch? I'm hungry!

Ravi loves to learn all about energy. After a cold lunch, he has a lot of questions about electricity.

Where does electricity come from?

What is electricity used for?

Will the power outage stop? I am still hungry for pizza!

Is electricity dangerous?

Professor Adams explains that electricity flows from one place to another along **wires**. This flow of electricity is called an electrical current. Electrical currents power the 3-D printer, the classroom lights, and more!

Electricity can be found in nature or made by humans.

You can see electricity when it comes from the sky as lightning!

SOLVE IT WITH SCIENCE!

Professor Adams tells the class that most electricity comes from **power plants**. There, electricity is made from other energy **sources**. Some power plants burn **fossil fuels**, such as coal and oil, to make electricity. Fossil fuels are nonrenewable. This means they will run out.

Burning fossil fuels creates, or makes, **pollution**. This school uses electricity from renewable energy sources.

Electricity is also made from renewable energy sources. They do not run out. Electricity from renewable energy sources is better for the environment. It creates less pollution. Below are four renewable energy sources.

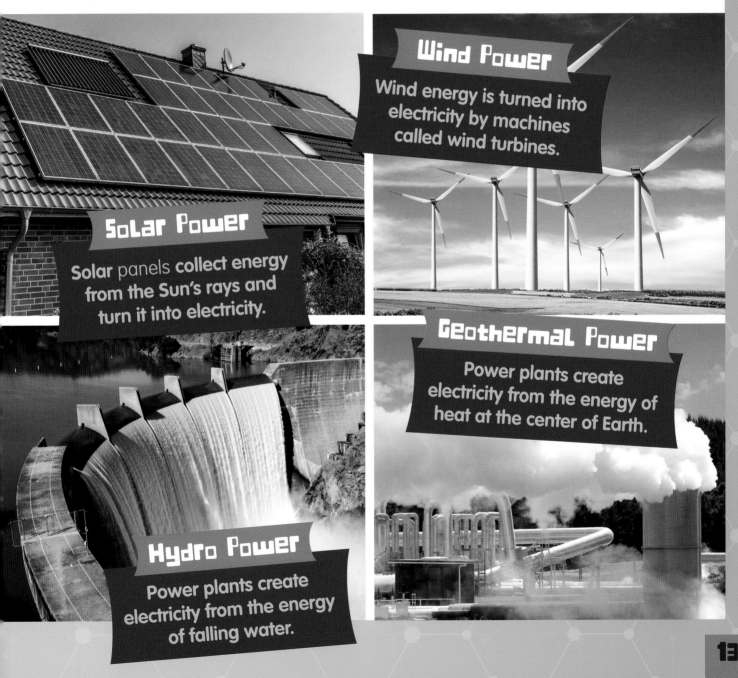

Wind Power

Wind energy is turned into electricity by machines called wind turbines.

Solar Power

Solar panels collect energy from the Sun's rays and turn it into electricity.

Geothermal Power

Power plants create electricity from the energy of heat at the center of Earth.

Hydro Power

Power plants create electricity from the energy of falling water.

Lewis explains that wires bring electricity from power plants into our homes and schools. Wires are made of materials called **conductors**. Electricity flows easily through conductors.

Copper is a conductor. Many wires are made of copper.

Wires have plastic on the outside to protect people from touching the conductor.

Wires bring electricity to an outlet in the wall. Then, machines such as 3-D printers are plugged into outlets and turned on. Touching a conductor is dangerous though. Electricity can pass from the conductor to the person, giving them an **electric shock**.

plug

Never put your fingers or other objects inside an outlet! Only plugs should go inside outlets. Talk to an adult about staying safe when using outlets.

outLet

POWER FROM BATTERIES

Bud-E doesn't get electricity from a wire. If he was plugged into an outlet in the wall, he wouldn't be able to move around! Bud-E gets the electricity he needs to work from a battery.

While I sleep, I plug my battery into an outlet. It gathers enough electricity for the day. This is called recharging.

Batteries hold electricity for an amount of time. Many objects, such as smartphones, cars, flashlights, and toys, use batteries. They come in all shapes and sizes.

Car batteries are large and shaped like rectangles.

Watch batteries are tiny and shaped like circles.

Keep old batteries in a clean container. Then bring them to a place where they can be handled safely.

BATTERIES ONLY

Some batteries cannot be recharged. They run out over time. It is important to safely throw away old batteries.

USING ELECTRICITY SAFELY

It is important to know how to be safe when using electricity.

Keep wires tidy so you don't trip over them.

Always ask an adult to change lightbulbs.

Keep objects that use electricity away from water. Make sure your hands are dry when you touch objects that use electricity.

Never put fingers or any other objects into outlets.

Never plug too many objects into one outlet.

Stay away from power wires and poles.

Electricity is very useful, but it can cause fires and give people shocks. Ask an adult to help you when you use electricity.

MAKING GOOD ENERGY CHOICES

We can help the environment by trying to use less energy, including electricity. Notice all of the ways you use electricity at home. Then, you can make choices to use less electricity. Here are some ways you can help.

When you are not using an object that runs on electricity, make sure it is turned off or unplugged. Remember to turn off lights when you leave a room!

Ask your parents to use energy-saving lightbulbs and machines at home. Try to use electricity only when you need to. For example, instead of using a dryer, your family could dry clothes by hanging them on a line.

Have a fun no-electricity night! Ask your parents or caregivers to light candles. You can do activities such as reading and playing games. Then, try to choose no-electricity activities more often in the future!

Hooray! The power outage is over. The time passed quickly while the classmates learned all about electricity! The lights come back on, and the 3-D printer whirrs and clicks. Thanks to electricity, there's pizza for everyone!

Remember to turn the 3-D printer off when it is not being used!

D printer

HOMEWORK

Sort these objects into those that use electricity from wires, and those that use batteries. Then, choose one object and explain how it can be used safely.

Toy Car

Remote Control

Hairdryer

Television

Smartwatch

Toaster

GLOSSARY

3-D PRINTER   A machine that creates 3-D objects, or objects with length, width, and height

CONDUCTORS   Materials or objects that allow electricity to flow through them

ELECTRIC SHOCK   A sudden flow of electricity through the body that can be painful and dangerous

FORCE   A push or pull that creates movement

FOSSIL FUELS   The remains of very old plants and animals that are burned to make energy

PANELS   Flat pieces that form a surface

POLLUTION   Harmful materials added to the environment

POWER PLANTS   Factories where electricity is created

SOURCES   Things or places where something begins

WIRE   A long, thin piece of metal used to carry electricity from one place to another

INDEX